Inhaling Grace

A 60-DAY UNHURRIED

LIVING DEVOTIONAL

by Alan Fadling

Published by Unhurried Living

Cover & interior design: Kirsten Doukas

Images: Paper Boats: © magann/lightstockphoto.com

ISBN-13: 978-1726041119
ISBN-10:1726041115

Printed in the United States of America

Inhaling Grace

OTHER BOOKS BY ALAN FADLING

An Unhurried Life

An Unhurried Leader

TO RICHARD E. FADLING

My father, who always modeled
a love of reading good books and imparted that love to me.
I dedicate this book to him in this his eightieth year.

TO WAYNE ANDERSON
(1940–2008)

With gratitude for his mentoring influence in my life,
showing me the way to live, serve, lead, and breathe deep in
the atmosphere of God's measureless grace.

CONTENTS

CONTENTS

CONTENTS

CONTENTS

FOREWORD

"Tell me about your life with God."

That's how my first spiritual director began our introductory meeting.

I stared at her, not sure how to respond. "Do you mean how I came to faith, or how I felt called to ministry, or . . .?"

"Anything you'd like to tell me about your life with God," she replied.

Not exactly the clarification I'd hoped for. So I answered in the only way I knew how: I spoke about being awakened to faith in Christ during college, being called to seminary, and being led into pastoral ministry. I also voiced my sense that God was leading me into something deeper in my life with him. But I didn't know what "deeper" meant.

When I finished sharing my story, I sat back in my seat and waited for her to assign me a spiritual discipline to practice. Wasn't that what spiritual directors were supposed to do? I expected her to suggest something grueling and unpleasant.

Like fasting. Instead, Diane surprised me by saying, "Sharon, what I hear in your story is this: you've taken so much care in your relationship with God and others. You've tried so hard to be faithful. Perhaps the Spirit is inviting you to relax into God's grace."

It wasn't the first time the Lord had spoken to me about my compulsions to define myself by my productivity and usefulness in the kingdom. Years before, God had revealed that the air I was breathing wasn't oxygen. Though I was giving lip service to grace, I was driven by anxiety and fear over whether I was being "faithful enough." My focus was on my faithfulness to God rather than God's faithfulness to me. What I needed was a radical conversion to grace, a deliverance from my perfectionist, workaholic tendencies. I needed to practice resting in my identity as God's beloved daughter. I needed to practice receiving the love of God, celebrating it, and then responding to the love that loved me—us—first.

That's the rhythm, always the rhythm: we receive from God; we respond to God. Like breathing. We inhale; we exhale. Sometimes, though, we get it backwards and end up hyperventilating because of all the energy we're exerting, trying to earn what God has so graciously given. It's God's faithfulness that inspires—literally, "breathes into"—and enables ours. It's the Good Shepherd who calls us by name and leads and guides us into paths of righteousness for his name's sake. We can rest in that. It's a good resting place. A joyful one.

But given our human tendency to drift toward fear, we need companions who help us stay rooted and grounded in the height and depth, length and breadth of the love of God perfectly revealed in Jesus Christ. We need people in our lives who ask penetrating questions and help us notice the ways we lean into striving rather than rest. We need people who are deeply attuned to the gentlest whispers of the Spirit, people who help us notice and name and inhale grace.

Alan Fadling is that sort of person. Alan is able to ask penetrating questions because he has heard the Spirit asking him such questions. And over the course of decades he has taken time to ponder and wrestle and respond. Alan is someone who gives voice to the truths we may be reluctant to name, and he does so with honesty, vulnerability, and wisdom. He has been radically converted to grace and has discovered the joy of being shepherded by a good and faithful God.

Through these daily reflections and questions, Alan invites us into the journey of keeping intimate company with Jesus, the journey of keeping in step with Jesus' unhurried rhythms of grace as he shepherds us into deeper, more abundant life and healing and freedom and transformation into his likeness. The journey takes us into deeper obedience and faithfulness, too. We're called to walk the narrow way, and that way is hard. But the path is graced.

So breathe deeply.

And enjoy the journey.

Sharon Garlough Brown
Author of the Sensible Shoes *series*

ACKNOWLEDGMENTS

I could not have completed this devotional without a community of friends to help me. For each one, I'm grateful.

First, I'm grateful to Scott and Steve Hutchison and the ministry of End Poverty Now (EPN), who funded an initial three-day retreat at a monastery in Central California so that I could gather and organize the hundred or more journal excerpts that formed the foundation of this project. EPN is a key partner with Unhurried Living, helping to fund our work through donated real estate, vehicles, and other valuable property. You can learn more about their work at donatecarsusa. org. These are dear friends.

I'm grateful to Lisa Guest who took those journal excerpts and created a first draft of this devotional. I found myself in the midst of another book project concurrently, and her work helped this project make immense progress.

A team of friends took time to review early drafts and provide immensely helpful feedback: Tom Talamantez, Cathy Huseby, Nancy Lopez, Matt Fogle, and of course, my beautiful bride, Gem. Amy Nemecek provided a final edit that caught and solved many issues in the manuscript. Any shortcomings that remain are my own, but this book is far better thanks to this helpful input.

I so appreciate the gift of Sharon Garlough Brown's foreword. I think you'll appreciate her honest, heartfelt story. I deeply resonate with it.

Finally, to John Welches and the team at Red Mallard. They provided so much help in the development, design, and layout of this project. I gave them the challenge of matching the quality of my two books with InterVarsity Press and they rose to it.

To any others who helped me in the project but whom I've overlooked, know that I'm still grateful even in my oversight.

INTRODUCTION

The grace of God is the atmosphere of his kingdom. We live by inhaling grace. We grow short of breath when we inhale anxiety, fear, or insecurity. These pollutants don't have a home in the joyful, generous kingdom of our Father in heaven. I wrote these sixty devotionals in hopes of helping you enjoy breathing more deeply in God's gracious presence.

These devotionals had their beginnings in my personal journal. I began to practice the regular discipline of spiritual journaling in 1990. Since then, I've written nearly ten thousand pages and over six million words in that journal. It's been a place of wrestling, thinking, reflection, and prayer. It's been a place of meeting with God. I hope it will be as fruitful for you to read these devotionals as it has been for me to write them.

A few years ago, a friend made it possible for me to get away for three days at a monastery near the Central California coast so I could go back through a few years of my journal to select excerpts for this first Unhurried Living devotional. The rolling, spring-green hills reached out into the distance, providing a vista that felt spacious to my soul. I didn't think of this collection being called *Inhaling Grace* back then, but I believe that is where the idea was planted.

As you read these entries, you'll probably notice frequent mention of some facet of Jesus as Good Shepherd. This theme emerged as these journal excerpts came together. For some, Jesus as Shepherd might feel overly familiar. Perhaps it brings to mind a traditional painting of Jesus with a lamb on his shoulders, making the metaphor feel old-fashioned and out-of-touch. I understand, but as one who has served as a pastor most of my adult life, the connection between Jesus as Shepherd and the work I do has been life-giving. In my training of Christian leaders, I remind them that they have a pastor—a Shepherd—in Jesus. And he is very good at what he does!

When I began my current spiritual journal nearly thirty years ago, my first entry captured my experience of a one-day solitude retreat that a future mentor, Wayne Anderson, was leading in Southern California. As part of a class of seminarians, we were given extended time to be alone in God's presence. It was only seventy-five minutes, but for many of us, it felt like forever. Most of us were hyperactive ministry leaders, and we were unaccustomed to spending much time alone or quiet. We thought of our relationship with God mostly in terms of our activity for God rather than our relationship with God.

The theme of that retreat day grew out of John 10 where Jesus calls himself the Good Shepherd. On page one of my journal, I wrote these notes: "Wayne taught from John 10, the Good Shepherd passage. It was gold! The three big ideas were that (1) we know Jesus in the same way that Jesus knows the Father, (2) we listen to Jesus, and (3) we follow Jesus. It is so simple, and yet so perspective changing." Can you sense the depths of grace in what I received that day?

Since that day, I've been on a journey of learning how to let myself be well-shepherded by Jesus in my life, my relationships, and my work. It's been a process of learning just how surrounded I am by grace, moment to moment, day to day. In the years since that first day practicing solitude and silence, I have continued this pattern. I've learned to follow Jesus into lonely places to pray (Luke 5:16). I've learned to inhale grace. Then my life, my words, and my works become an exhaling of grace.

It's my prayer that as you read these entries you'll experience a renewal and refreshing of your ideas, assumptions, expectations, and perspectives of Jesus. I hope you'll see how he is wanting to guide you into more and more life. I'm hopeful that you'll become more accustomed to inhaling the grace of God that is always with you. I'm glad we get to inhale his grace together.

KNOWING AND BEING KNOWN BY THE SHEPHERD

"I am the good shepherd. I know my own and my own know me, just as the Father knows me and I know the Father; and I lay down my life for the sheep." — John 10:14-15 ESV

Jesus is the Good Shepherd, and he is my Good Shepherd. He knows me; I know him. This mutual knowing—facilitated by the Spirit—is similar to the knowledge the Son and the Father have of one another.

The Father and the Son share the closest imaginable union with one another, and I am invited to such a union with my Good Shepherd. The Scriptures use the human example of the closeness of a husband and a wife to describe just how close our union with the Father and the Son could actually be. This is a wondrous reality that takes time to sink in. Embracing this invitation—loving God with all your heart, mind, soul, and strength and investing in your relationship with him—

can change your life. You can remember that your life here on earth is already an eternal life.

I'm humbled, grateful, and amazed by this opportunity for intimacy with my God. I am further humbled as I consider that Jesus' death on the cross is what has opened the way for me to come so freely and confidently into God's presence.

- *What does it mean to you that Jesus is your Good Shepherd?*

- *What do you do regularly to strengthen your relationship with Jesus and grow closer to him?*

THE SHEPHERD'S VOICE

"The sheep hear his voice, and he calls his own sheep
by name and leads them out. When he has brought
out all his own, he goes before them, and the sheep
follow him, for they know his voice."
— John 10:3–4 ESV

"They know his voice." It's a simple phrase, but I was especially touched when I read it this time: they know his voice. We learn to recognize the voice of another as we spend time with that person. If we spend enough time with them, we will at some point be able to pick their voice out of a crowd. When my wife, Gem, and I are at a large event, I know her voice, and I easily recognize her laugh from across the room.

So how do you and I come to know the voice of the Spirit that well? We don't want to miss him when he speaks in the depths of our souls. I've come to recognize his voice in large part because of my time reading the Scriptures. I've read and studied them long enough that I recognize that same Voice when I hear it rising up within my soul.

I don't listen to the Spirit's voice as merely a recreational activity, though. What God says is life! I'm not following a stranger but a Friend.

Wouldn't it be beautiful if more of Jesus' sheep came to fully recognize their Shepherd's voice?

- *What will you do to become more familiar with—and able to recognize—God's voice?*

- *What do you do—or whom can you turn to—when you think you've heard God's guiding voice but aren't sure?*

GUIDED BY MY SHEPHERD

I will fear no evil, for you are with me; your rod and
your staff, they comfort me. — *Psalm 23:4 ESV*

Psalm 23 may be one of the most well-known passages of Scripture. Its words of comfort are familiar to many, perhaps especially at funerals. But Psalm 23 has much to say for every stage of our lives.

We read, for instance, "He guides me along the right paths for his name's sake" (v. 3 NIV). My Good Shepherd has it in his heart to guide me along the very best paths because his good care for me reflects well on him. Just as I want my own sons to live well because it says something about how I've served them as a father, so the Lord shepherds me away from rutted, empty, wayward paths and toward nourishing, refreshing, fulfilling ones.

Even those best paths, however, will take me through dark seasons. Darkness can come with losses such as a prodigal child, a chronic illness, divorce, job loss, aging parents, or the death of someone close to us.

I'm guessing you're like me: I would rather never walk through dark valleys. But since I must at times walk through such places, I am grateful I'm not walking alone. My Good Shepherd guides me, protects me from evil, and brings me comfort when I'm tempted to give in to anxiety, fear, doubt, or insecurity.

Finally, consider the image in verse 5 of this psalm: "You prepare a table before me in the presence of my enemies." Of course, I'd prefer sharing a sumptuous feast with my friends; but when my enemies threaten my joy, my gracious Host provides a place of hospitality for me. I enjoy the Shepherd's goodness in the presence of evil. I can then share that goodness in ways that might even overcome evil. Trust this reality today.

- *Spend some time thanking your Good Shepherd for guiding you along right paths.*

- *Confess to him any fears of evil. Talk to him about whatever darkness you're dealing with.*

- *Ask him to help you become aware of his presence with you.*

I LACK NOTHING

*The LORD is my shepherd, I lack nothing....Surely
your goodness and love will follow me all the days
of my life, and I will dwell in the house of the LORD
forever. — Psalm 23:1, 6 NIV*

As I read these verses—the first and last lines of Psalm 23—I am struck by how they speak to the general sense of dread that something bad is about to happen. I have often felt I live in a world that sometimes feels unsafe and threatening. These feelings are like an echo of something old; they are not feelings rooted in adult realities. I didn't know Jesus as my Shepherd for the first seventeen years of my life. Instead, I experienced a world where I felt I lacked much and where worry and abandonment seemed to follow me all the time.

But now I know that I live in a world where Jesus personally shepherds me. There is nothing that I truly need that he does not provide. All that I desire I find in him and receive from him. And if I'm being followed, it's by his goodness and love, and this will be true for eternity. I will always have a home in

God's presence, and this reality is quite a contrast to beliefs formed in my childhood and experienced in emotions I still carry around as an adult.

I want to keep growing in this healthy, wholesome reality. I want to work together with my Good Shepherd as he replaces my childhood leftovers of angst, insecurity, fear, anxiety, and self-doubt. I want to trust Jesus more deeply and rely on God's goodness and love following me, surrounding me always.

- *What does it mean to you—despite the challenges you face right now—that God's goodness and love are with you and "will follow [you] all the days of [your] life"?*

- *What in your life does "The Lord is my shepherd, I lack nothing" cause you to see differently?*

GROWING UP IN THE PRESENCE OF THE LORD, PART 1

Meanwhile, the boy Samuel grew up in the presence of the LORD. — 1 Samuel 2:21 NIV

I love that Samuel "grew up in the presence of the LORD." And I find myself wishing I had grown up in the presence of the Lord rather than growing up with little awareness of God and the truth that he is with me. I can only imagine how different my childhood and youth might have been had I known my Good Shepherd.

That said, I am grateful that I have grown up in the presence of the Lord over the years of my adult life. I'm grateful for this growth.

As we grow up in the presence of the Lord, we may find ourselves being approved of less and less by the world and without a lot of company. The same was true in Samuel's day. Eli's sons, who are described as "worthless men" (2:12), "treated the offering of the LORD with contempt" (2:17). Yet as Eli's own sons were walking away from God, young Samuel was growing up in the Lord's presence.

Whether you have been aware of God's presence from childhood or have become a friend of God later in life, you are growing up, even now, in the presence of God. What a fertile place to grow and develop.

- *During your childhood and youth, who among your friends and acquaintances might have led you on the path away from God?*

- *What did God do to put you and keep you on the path toward growing into a Christlike individual? Whom did he use in your life?*

GROWING UP IN THE PRESENCE OF THE LORD, PART 2

*The LORD was gracious to Hannah; she gave birth
to three sons and two daughters. Meanwhile, the boy
Samuel grew up in the presence of the LORD.*
— 1 Samuel 2:21 NIV

The Lord was gracious to Samuel as he grew up at the temple in the presence of the Lord and under the guidance of Eli the priest. The Lord was also gracious to Hannah, giving her five more children after she—true to her word—gave up her first-born to the Lord's service.

I cannot imagine what it would be like to give up a child. What if after you had prayed so long for a child, you had to give him up to be raised at a distant monastery? This is essentially what Hannah does with Samuel. How would you feel if your firstborn son had grown up among the monks and you only saw him once a year? You'd be proud of his service to God, but you'd miss him terribly.

And yet, this is much like what God himself did with his Son. In love, God gave us the gift of his Son. Jesus grew up in a world that didn't understand him or recognize him for who he actually was. He grew up in the presence of his Father for our sake. What a remarkable gift. What a wonderful invitation.

- *What has God asked you to offer up for him?*

- *What blessings have come in the wake of your sacrifice and obedience?*

WHAT ARE YOU THINKING ABOUT?

We ponder your steadfast love, O God, in the midst of your temple. — Psalm 48:9 NRSV

What words come to mind when you think about God's love?

Maybe some of these: reliable, trustworthy, eternal, redemptive, transformative, undeserved, unearned, gracious. The list could go on, making it clear that God's love is something for us to think about long and deep. The more we do, the more we marvel.

God loves you and me in ways that I can't begin to fathom. We need only look at the cross: "God demonstrates His own love toward us, in that while we were still sinners, Christ died for us" (Romans 5:8 NKJV). Psalm 139 tells us that we are "fearfully and wonderfully made" (v. 14), and Jesus even numbers the hair on our heads (Matthew 10:30).

But do I really trust that God is love? My behavior has sometimes suggested—or perhaps even shouted—that I don't. Can that change? Can I grow to trust that God really is love? Of course I can, if I want to! Though I may never fully comprehend the measureless height, depth, length, and breadth of God's affection, his delight in me, or his availability to me, I can explore these realities more deeply than I have so far. So can you. We can make pondering our Good Shepherd's steadfast love part of a regular engagement with God day by day.

- *When did God's love for you first become real? Reflect on and describe the moment.*

- *What, if anything, tempts you not to deeply trust that God is love?*

TWO LITTLE COINS

A poor widow came and put in two small copper
coins, which make a penny. — Mark 12:42 ESV

"It is true that it is only within our power to give two mites, our time and our desire; but the Son of God held that the gift of the widow, though it was worth less than a farthing, was the best of the offerings made to God, since it was all that she had." *

These words resonate in my soul. Ward suggests that the currency we have to invest in our spiritual progress is our time and our desire. Maybe we feel that our time and desire are small, like the widow's two small coins. But Jesus sees and values our little offering. He knows its value because he knows our hearts and our intentions when we pray.

So when I'm praying, what am I intending or desiring? I may be intending to fulfill some religious duty that I believe a

---

* Reginald Somerset Ward, *A Guide for Spiritual Directors* (London: A. R. Mowbray, 1957), p. 71.

Christian should satisfy. I might be acting out of empty habit. Perhaps I'm on autopilot, going through the motions and unable to remember the last time my prayer was a time of Jesus filling my heart and touching my soul.

Instead, I can respond to God from love rather than duty. I can pray from a whole heart. I can offer honest words to the God who is actually present—my love, my praise, my affection, and my grateful acknowledgment of God's grace.

- *What do you do—or might you do—to keep prayer alive, to approach it as a life-giving conversation with God and not a mere duty?*

- *Consider finding a prayer partner with whom you can pray—together or over the phone—at least once a week. Try it for a while and see its impact on your prayer life.*

PRAYER: GOD-FOCUSED OR ME-FOCUSED?

Oh give thanks to the LORD, for he is good; for his steadfast love endures forever! — Psalm 118:1 ESV

It is daunting to stop and consider that we pray to the eternal, holy, all-powerful God of the entire universe and of all history. Understandably, being in his glorious presence can make us hyperaware of our sins, our failings, our shortcomings. All too easily, then, we become focused not on God but on ourselves, specifically on the ways we are far from being the person God wants us to be.

Reginald Somerset Ward offers this wise counsel:

> *The effect on prayer of constant absorption in the negative is to fix the inward gaze of the person on every failure in concentration and attention as a sin and as of more importance than the prayer itself, until at last the whole activity of prayer is swallowed up by introspection and the person sinks ever deeper into a spiritual bog of depression.... In such cases it is best to fix for the person a period in the rule of prayer which is to be entirely given up to thanksgivings.**

Are you familiar with such self-focused orientation in prayer? I am. I can too often be a "cup-half-empty" person, and my prayer then becomes a running apology for my failures of attention, faithfulness, or self-discipline.

Somerset-Ward recommends that we enjoy a period of thanksgiving every time we go before God in prayer. There have been seasons when I needed thanksgiving to be my primary form of prayer. I've found it helpful to return to thanksgiving every time I notice my confession in prayer becoming self-condemning. Turning my focus again on my good and gracious God brings refreshment as well as the desire to keep praying. Gratitude is exhaling the grace I'm inhaling.

- *Why do you think prayer can sometimes become a lot of apologizing, recounting failure, and being down on ourselves?*

- *Find a go-to psalm of thanksgiving that you can quickly turn to when your prayer becomes a litany of your shortcomings and wrongdoings. Take a look, for instance, at Psalm 30, Psalm 92, Psalm 100, or Psalm 145.*

* *A Guide for Spiritual Directors*, p. 54

PRAYER:
PEOPLE-FOCUSED OR
THING-FOCUSED?

Pray for one another....The prayer of a righteous person has great power. — *James 5:16 ESV*

What should we pray about? Whom should we pray for?

To answer those questions, we need to discern what we genuinely and presently care about. We can ask ourselves who we want to be more caring toward. We can pray from a place of genuine care for any event, concern, or person. Our list can be mostly focused on people in our life: family, neighbors, co-workers, and so on. When we choose this perspective—when we consider prayer an opportunity to give attention to what and who matter to us—we may desire to pray more.

When my prayers are mostly about things coming up in my calendar or on my to-do list, I often end up feeling like I'm praying only about selfish concerns: I want this appointment to be successful and well-received; I want people to like what

I planned; I want the outcome of my current task to reflect well on me. That's not bad as far as it goes, but it doesn't go far enough. May our foremost prayers come to reflect the servant heart of our Shepherd for the good of those we serve. And a good place to start is to pray for those people first.

- *Do you struggle to keep your prayers focused on the people impacted by your plans and your work? If so, why do you think this is?*

- *What specific aspects of an upcoming task, appointment, or event (and the people involved) can you bring into God's presence in prayer?*

PRAYING FOR OTHERS

"Whoever believes in me, as the Scripture has said,
'Out of his heart will flow rivers of living water.'"
— *John 7:38 ESV*

When I'm not taking much time to pray for the people God has placed in my life, I find that my prayerlessness affects my interactions with them and my thoughts about them. To be specific, I notice my empty heart: I don't find much holy concern for their souls or genuine interest in their spiritual growth. I don't even feel much joyful attraction to them or much real desire to spend time with them.

But when I am praying often and well for other people, I experience something like what Jesus spoke about in today's verse. I actually experience his living water flowing through me. As a result, I find myself very much concerned about their souls and their spiritual growth, and I want to spend more time with them—for their good more than for my own.

So, in terms of kingdom influence, investing time in praying for all the people in my life increases my kingdom energy and my kingdom awareness when I'm with them. I find myself wanting to bless, help, encourage, and invite them more deeply into God's kingdom purposes.

Try an experiment: Choose someone in your life—in your workplace or at church, in your neighborhood, or even in your family—whom you find hard to love right now. Then pray for this person regularly for two weeks. At the end of two weeks, watch for how your heart has changed as a result of your praying.

- *Do you know of anyone who has prayed for you? If possible, thank that person and offer some specific evidence of the positive impact their prayers had on your life.*

SENT FORTH IN PEACE

*Jesus said, "Peace be with you! As the Father has sent
me, I am sending you." And with that he breathed on
them and said, "Receive the Holy Spirit."*
— John 20:21–22 NIV

Jesus wants you and me to have his peace when he sends us
out into a world that knows little of true peace. At best, peace
in this world is mostly about the absence of obvious conflict
in our hearts or in our relationships. At worst, a lack of peace
means people are at odds with one another in heartbreaking
ways.

It would appear that the means by which Jesus gives his peace
to his followers is by breathing his own breath onto them: Jesus gives us his Holy Spirit. My body breathes in air and lives.
My soul breathes in God's Spirit and lives.

Our physical breathing is involuntary. We have more of a
choice when it comes to our spiritual breathing: Will we acknowledge Jesus as our Lord and thereby receive (inhale) his
Spirit? And when we are following Jesus, will we yield to him

every morning, breathing in his Holy Spirit in fresh ways and asking him, the Good Shepherd, to lead us through the day for the Father's purposes? Living in the power and energy of God's Spirit brings us into a life of more joyful service that has eternal value.

- *What makes the peace Jesus wants to breathe into you elusive? What could you do to welcome the breath of God's Spirit within you?*

- *Reflect on a time when you experienced the power and energy of God's Spirit. Thank him for making a difference, and spend some time enjoying his presence with you now.*

FINANCIAL FARMING

"Go! I am sending you out like lambs among wolves.
Do not take a purse or bag or sandals; ... for the
worker deserves his wages." — Luke 10:3–4, 7 NIV

Early in his ministry, Jesus spoke these words to about seventy of his followers as he sent them into the surrounding towns and villages to do what he had been doing and say what he had been saying. Clearly, such ministry would require them to trust God. Then Jesus added a little twist. They weren't to take any food or money with them. They were to trust God not only for ministry opportunities and changed lives, but also for food, water, and a place to sleep.

Later, however, on the last night of their earthly time together, Jesus said something different.

> *He said to them, "When I sent you out without a purse, bag, or sandals, did you lack anything?" They said, "No, not a thing." He said to them, "But now, the one who has a purse must take it, and likewise a bag. And the one who has no sword must sell his cloak and buy one." (Luke 22:35–36 NRSV)*

As I think about my own journey in ministry, for many years I went where God called without carrying along obvious stores of funding—and I never lacked anything. Later on in my ministry, I came to believe that greater intentionality and initiative in managing our finances was God's invitation. I sensed it was a movement toward maturity in my way of working with God in life and ministry.

In what kind of life season do you find yourself? Is it a time for travelling light and trusting God's provision moment to moment? Or is it a time for strategic initiatives and wise investments to provide for your present and your future?

- *It can be tempting to stay in an old way of relating to money when a new way is necessary. Is God calling you to change something about your own financial farming?*

- *Think about the different seasons of money management in your life. Answer Jesus' question: "Did you lack anything?" What kind of financial farming season are you in now?*

- *Stewardship is caring for resources belonging to another. Explain this concept of stewardship in your own words as it applies in your own life. How has this idea impacted your financial farming through the years?*

WORDS THAT BLESS, PART 1

Let the words of my mouth and the meditation of my heart be acceptable in your sight, O LORD, my rock and my redeemer. — Psalm 19:14 ESV

Watching television news has been so painful lately. I'm thinking specifically about the words being used and the way they are spoken. So much conflict, so many harsh words, so many accusations and insults make the headlines. Too many people speak to others with disrespect and contempt. A gracious and honoring word seems hard to come by.

All this has made me think that, as a culture, it would be so helpful to rediscover the language of blessing. I'm not talking about saying a prayer before you eat. Not that kind of blessing. I don't just mean having your pastor say something encouraging at the end of a service. Blessing is not empty, cotton-candy language.

Blessing is speaking words of substantial goodness to one another that actually bring about that goodness in another's life. That's worth saying again: I'm talking about speaking words that bring real goodness and blessing to another.

I've learned a lot over the years about the power of blessing—especially spoken blessing. Hearing words of blessing spoken over us gives those words greater power. You are invited to hear words of blessing from your Good Shepherd. You are invited to share those good words with those who cross your path. What a difference you could make in your world!

- *What are some powerful words of blessing—words of substantial goodness—that have been spoken over you? If you don't have many such memories, take time to read Psalm 139 and be blessed.*

- *As you look around you, where is blessing needed? Who is one person you could meet with, call, or write to offer some heartfelt words of blessing? When do you want to do that?*

WORDS THAT BLESS, PART 2

*May our sons in their youth be like plants full
grown.... May our barns be filled with produce of
every kind.... May there be no breach in the walls,
no exile, and no cry of distress in our streets.... Happy
are the people whose God is the LORD.*
— *Psalm 144:12–15 NRSV*

I love these lines, these words of blessing. Did you notice that they are not just "me" prayers but "us" prayers? These blessings are wishes for robust life, great abundance, and protection from real harm.

These blessings also got me thinking about what blessings I want to pray for the good of my family, my friends, my community, my nation. Here are a handful that came to mind:

May you bless every desire in our hearts to do good in honor of your kingdom.

May our families seek you first, Lord God, in everything we do.

May our next season be one of recovering whatever the locusts have eaten in the last ones.

May we know deep peace, abounding joy, boundless love, and holy power in our lives.

May we see you and your ways even more clearly than we have so far.

May we be as carefree in heart and mind as the birds in our backyards. May we, like them, simply trust that you, our Good Shepherd, will care for us day by day. Amen.

- *Where are you feeling a need for blessing in your own life? If God were to speak timely words of blessing over you, what would you like to hear?*

- *Take time to formulate words of blessing for you and your family, for you and your church, and/or for you and your community.*

A RIVER OF LIVING WATER

I will pour out my spirit on all flesh; your sons and
your daughters shall prophesy, your old men shall
dream dreams, and your young men shall see visions.
Even on the male and female slaves, in those days, I
will pour out my spirit. — Joel 2:28–29 NRSV

This word that Joel spoke for the Lord is fulfilled after the resurrection and ascension of Jesus, on the day of Pentecost. And it is fulfilled for us today. Our bodies ("all flesh") become temples of God's Holy Spirit as we welcome Jesus' reign in our lives. And God's presence within us—his Spirit—enables us to see in a limited way from his divine and eternal perspective ("see visions"); to dream in line with God's heart and mind ("dream dreams"); and to speak words of blessing and truth to people on God's behalf ("prophesy").

This beautiful outcome is not limited merely to young, virile men. Sons and daughters will further God's kingdom in creative ways. Old men will participate alongside young. The socially low on the ladder ("slaves") will have as much king-dom authority as any "somebody" does. God is not nearly as interested in our status in the world as we are.

Instead, it is God's design that every person might receive so much of his poured-out Spirit that their winsomeness, grace, and love would be like a river of living water flowing from within them. God's Spirit can and does make this happen, and he does not use the same criteria for selecting candidates as we do.

- *What encouragement for your spiritual community do you find in these verses from Joel?*

- *Who did you think of when you read the words "winsome-ness, grace, and love"? What does that person's life model for you?*

A GREAT CLOUD OF WITNESSES

Since we are surrounded by so great a cloud of witnesses, let us also lay aside every weight and the sin that clings so closely, and let us run with perseverance the race that is set before us, looking to Jesus the pioneer and perfecter of our faith.
— Hebrews 12:1–2 NRSV

What do you picture when you read that you, as a follower of Jesus, are "surrounded by so great a cloud of witnesses"? I picture something even greater than a stadium filled with 100,000 fans cheering for their home team. Imagine a thousand such stadiums, and that cloud of witnesses is still far smaller than the one described in Hebrews.

We can be glad to be surrounded by this cloud. All the faithful who have gone before us testify of the blessings of living life with and for Jesus. They would probably also tell us how much they wish they had set aside every burden and distracting shortcoming sooner.

May we learn from these godly people and "look to Jesus" with a laser-focused single-mindedness. Jesus, our Good Shepherd, invites us to know the joy that satisfies, the joy that can help us endure whatever suffering may come. Paul compared us to the elite athlete who looks past the pain of training to the goal of peak performance and its prize (see 1 Cor. 9:24-27).

We will know the pain of training in Christlikeness, but remember that we are not running for a temporary reward or fleeting praise. Ours is an eternal reward of abiding in the very presence of God's loving favor.

Jesus will coach us in this race as much as we'll let him. As we run this race, he is right alongside us.

- *Name some forerunners of the faith who are especially encouraging to you. Consider the saints you know or have known in person, the saints from church history through the years, and the saints in the Scriptures.*

- *To whom might you be a witness? Who might you encourage in their faith? What are they seeing in you about life lived with and for Jesus? What do you want them to see?*

THE WORK OF GOD...
REDEFINED

"This is the work of God, that you believe in him
whom he has sent." — John 6:29 ESV

What comes to mind when you hear the phrase "work of God"? When Jesus' disciples asked essentially that same question, he didn't answer with a to-do list, or an inventory of personal qualifications, or a list of required courses and specific accomplishments at the local synagogue. Instead, Jesus responded with an invitation to trust that he was indeed sent by God.

Often during Jesus' earthly ministry, people asked for a sign to believe in; they wanted him to do something spectacular that only God could do. Jesus did plenty of healings, miracles, and powerful teachings—and still not everyone believed. In this passage, and several times throughout the gospels, Jesus did not give a checklist to potential followers. What Jesus did was invite them to believe in him and to trust him. But this answer wasn't at all what everyone expected.

Doing God's work on this earth involves more fully trusting Jesus as our Savior, following him as our King, and loving him more and more with all that is in us. This is the point at which all true work for God begins. Jesus redefined the very nature of the work of God, and he invites us to join him in this very good work.

- *Why is Jesus' call to simply believe in him such a challenge for some of us? Wherever you are on your journey with the Shepherd, how have you been learning to trust him more and more?*

- *Think of a time when your Good Shepherd gave you an unexpected answer to a question, an unexpected change of direction in your life, or an unexpected resolution to a difficult situation. What wisdom have you seen in this unexpected input?*

SOUL NOURISHMENT

"I am the bread of life. Whoever comes to me will
never be hungry again. Whoever believes in me will
never be thirsty." — John 6:35 NLT

What a beautiful promise the Shepherd makes to us, the sheep
of his flock!

Jesus is the one who truly satisfies our hunger and thirst. He
was blunt in proclaiming this truth: those who trust in him
will never be hungry or thirsty again. His words sound a lot
like the first verse of Psalm 23: "The LORD is my shepherd; I
shall not want." We are in the care of a Good Shepherd. We
are not needy, but watched over.

If I'm honest, however, even since I began to trust in Jesus—
and to entrust myself to him—I have experienced plenty of
moments when I've felt hungry or thirsty in soul. But that reality doesn't prove Jesus wrong at all. It simply says that I'm
still learning to fully trust him. I know from experience that
when I choose to trust Jesus and rest in him, he thoroughly
meets all my soul needs.

Jesus—and only Jesus—truly nourishes and satisfies a hungry and thirsty soul. Do you long to more fully receive this soul nourishment today?

- *Explain what your soul gets hungry and thirsty for...and why Jesus is the bread that meets those needs and satisfies your soul.*

- *What keeps you from receiving the soul nourishment that Jesus longs to give you?*

WHY DOES GOD BLESS YOU?

"I will make of you a great nation, and I will bless you, and make your name great, so that you will be a blessing." — Genesis 12:2 NRSV

The words above are God's blessing to Abraham when he called this wealthy son of an idol worshiper to leave his father's house, all that was familiar, and to obediently go to... well, God didn't tell him where. God's command to leave came with a promise but not with an itinerary. Abraham was obedient despite the vague instructions, and of course God was faithful and kept this promise.

But notice the heart of that promise. Like Abraham, I am blessed not just so that *I'll* be blessed; I am blessed so that God's blessing will flow to others through me. My friend Todd Hunter, an Anglican bishop, has been reminding me that I am blessed *for the sake of others.*

Of course I want to be blessed. We all do. But I also truly want to bless others. I want others to receive the good things from me and through me that I've received from a generous Father.

Most recently, though, what I've needed to do is *let myself be blessed*. I have resisted God's blessing because I focus on whether or not I *deserve* to be blessed. That's really the wrong question. God isn't assessing whether or not I deserve his generosity. He is simply generous. This is how God treats us. It is rooted in him, not in us. God would love nothing more than for you and me to open ourselves fully to all the ways he desires to be generous. Doesn't that sound inviting?

- *Think about God's blessings in your life. In what way do these blessings enable you to bless others? Think of a few examples.*

- *Give an example of someone you have seen blessing others with the blessings God has given them. If you've been one of those on the receiving end of their blessing, share how God is glorified in the actions of this person.*

TESTING JESUS OR FOLLOWING HIM? PART 1

"Why does this generation ask for a sign?"
— Mark 8:12 NIV

In Jesus' day, people wanted him to give them a sign to prove his identity. We also live in a generation that wants a sign, a generation that seems more interested in exciting happenings than in walking through life in relationship with Jesus. Yet Jesus' own life—his actions, his interactions with people, his character—are more than enough evidence of his identity as God's Son. There is no need for an outward sign or more amazing miracles. The way Jesus lived, what he did, how and what he taught—it all points to the truth that he is God's Son.

Yet the Pharisees approached Jesus, "asking him for a sign from heaven, to test him" (Mark 8:11 NRSV). The Pharisees were experts in the Torah as well as the oral tradition that grew up around it. They were among the Jewish ruling class. They put great emphasis on following both the law and tradition. They weren't interested in trusting Jesus or following him. They wanted to stand at a distance, test him, and assess him.

They were unwilling to come to him, listen to him, and learn whether or not he could be trusted. With hard hearts and closed minds, they were testing Jesus, and they were only going to see what they wanted to see. It's always helpful for me to graciously and gently ask myself, "Why am I coming to God right now? Am I coming in response to his invitation, or am I coming with some personal agenda?" God cares about our concerns and welcomes us to bring them to him. He also wants us to learn how trustworthy his purposes are and to come with a receptive, attentive heart.

- *Can you think of times or ways when you were tempted to test God? Perhaps a conversation with a good friend could help you notice this in your story.*

- *When we are talking with people whose hearts are hard and whose minds are closed, how might we talk about our faith in Jesus, our relationship with him, or his role as Good Shepherd in a way that might tantalize them?*

TESTING JESUS OR FOLLOWING HIM? PART 2

Come close to God, and God will come close to you.
— James 4:8 NLT

It always helps me to remember that prayer is a relationship I'm cultivating more than a discipline I'm practicing. Sometimes, to help myself enter into this reality, I imagine myself having a conversation with Jesus. Below is a prayerful conversation I had about waking up to ways I'd been testing God rather than following God.

Me: Jesus, I realize I'm like the Pharisees, guilty of testing you rather than drawing close to you.

Jesus: I understand why you keep your distance, and those reasons aren't rooted in truth. You are afraid of some distorted image of me that you haven't yet let go of. You are anxious that I will somehow fail to provide what you need. You could be free of fear and worry if you trusted me.

Me: I hear your invitation to trust you. I know you call your-self my Good Shepherd, and I want to trust you. I want to believe that I am not alone, that you will never abandon me, and that yours is a kingdom of abundance. Open my eyes to see. Open my ears to listen. Open my heart to trust. I am willing to follow you—and follow you closely.

Jesus: I'm happy you're choosing to follow me. Be ready. Be attentive. Trust me. You have my help.

When you think about prayer today, imagine Jesus welcoming you into his presence. Envision his great interest, deep concern, and availability to encourage you and guide you in your life and work today.

- *What lies—regarding your sense of worth, an inaccurate picture of God, distrust, even anger at God—are keeping you standing at a distance from Jesus rather than entering into conversation with him?*

- *What role can and does the Holy Spirit play in our commitment to follow Jesus as our Good Shepherd, to live with him as Lord, and to serve him, our Savior, with gratitude?*

FOLLOWING JESUS:
TWO OPTIONS

A large crowd kept following him, because they saw
the signs that he was doing for the sick. Jesus went up
the mountain and sat down there with his disciples.
— John 6:2–3 NRSV

The apostle John is straightforward about why the crowd was following Jesus. Rather than desiring to learn from this wise and compassionate Rabbi so they could teach others, the crowd wanted to see something exciting happen. They wanted to be there when Jesus did his next miracle. They wanted to be able to say that they were there to witness it.

Why do I follow Jesus? Maybe it is because of something exciting I expect him to do. Or perhaps I follow him because he actually knows the way—because he actually is the way (John 14:6)—to life.

Is my motive closer to that of the crowd, or is my heart like that of a disciple who sits with Jesus and learns from him in order to better follow him? Am I seeking stimulation or transformation?

The crowd generally follows at a distance. Disciples follow Jesus closely.

- *How would you describe the closeness of your following Jesus these days? In what ways are you following closely? In what ways are you wandering or even avoiding him? Reflect on your answer.*

- *Whatever the distance, how might you come to follow Jesus more closely today?*

THE LIGHT OF HIS PRESENCE

[Jesus] said this to test [Philip], for [Jesus] himself knew what he was going to do. — John 6:6 NRSV

Jesus had just asked Philip, "Where are we to buy bread for these people to eat?" (John 6:5 NRSV). From a human perspective, feeding such a huge crowd was an overwhelming, if not utterly impossible, task. How would the disciples come up with enough cash to feed these thousands of people? Who nearby would even have that much food to sell?

In the back of my mind, I'm tempted to think that Jesus said what he did as kind of a trick question for Philip. But Jesus isn't trying to trick us. He does test us, though. And testing brings to the surface dynamics that are actually present but perhaps unseen: in this case, does Philip trust Jesus? While the thought of being tested by Jesus may seem threatening, remember that whatever surfaces—a lack of faith, for instance—can be transformed once it is brought into the light of his presence.

Jesus knows what is going on in my life. When I feel he is testing me, I can be confident that he is not asking me trick questions. Instead, he wants me to be more mindful of our relationship and more aware of exactly who he is. He always does this from a motive of love. He wants to bring healing to what is unwell, restoration to what is broken, and cleansing to what has been dirtied.

- *When, if ever, have you felt like God asked you a trick question? Now that you can look back at those circumstances, how might that moment have been a test designed to bring to the surface something in you that you needed to see?*

- *Think of a time when the Holy Spirit brought something to the surface that had been unseen. Once it was in the light of Jesus' presence, what transformation occurred?*

SEEKING FIRST

"Seek the Kingdom of God above all else, and live righteously, and he will give you everything you need." — Matthew 6:33 NLT

I once heard a pastor say that the choices between good and bad are often easy to see, but the choices between good and better can be more difficult. I've thought about that often. It's easy for me to decide to go to church on Sunday morning instead of staying home and watching television. It's harder to know sometimes whether I should read a good book or look for an opportunity to serve a neighbor in need.

Every day we face choices between good and bad as well as choices between good and better. Jesus' words in Matthew 6:33 can help us deal with both types of decisions: "Seek the Kingdom of God above all else."

It can be easy to spend big blocks of time and enormous energy on secondary things when we approach them as though they are primary. What is primary? Jesus calls us to love God with all we are and to love our neighbors as ourselves (Matt.

22:37-39). In today's verse he calls us to seek God's kingdom above all else. The two ideas are related, and both require us to make our relationship with God primary. Only then can we live and influence out of being filled by God's love. That's just what everyone needs.

- *Consider a typical day or week in your life. What minors are you tempted to major in? In other words, how are you living (or not living) in keeping with the priority of loving God and loving your neighbor? What changes do you wish to make? How might a mentor help?*

- *What do you do regularly—or what might you do more regularly—to remember God's love for you that would refresh you and empower you to love others?*

WELCOMING GOD INTO OUR WEAKNESS AND FAILURE

When I saw [the risen Jesus], I fell at his feet as
though dead. Then he placed his right hand on me
and said: "Do not be afraid. I am the First and the
Last. I am the Living One; I was dead, and now look,
I am alive for ever and ever! And I hold the keys of
death and Hades." — Revelation 1:17–18 NIV

The last of Jesus' twelve disciples to die, the apostle John wrote
that he had been exiled to the island of Patmos by Rome "because of the word of God and the testimony of Jesus" (Rev. 1:9
NIV). John had been preaching about the resurrected Jesus,
so a testy Roman government sent him to Patmos where he
would be preaching to no one.

While John was on Patmos, the resurrected Jesus appeared
to him, and John "fell at his feet as though dead." I probably
would have fainted, too, had I seen this vision of the glorified
Jesus who spoke to the terrified apostle: "Do not be afraid."

Jesus speaks similar words of courage, peace, and empowerment to help us in our life and in our work. Even though it is work that I do imperfectly, it is work that Jesus has given me and is continually training me in.

I am keenly aware of my weaknesses and failures. I never want those to detract from the purposes of God in and through me. I invite you to join me in these intentions: I will focus on God's great faithfulness, on the power he offers me when he calls me to a task, and on listening for his guidance.

- *List two or three personal weaknesses you tend to dwell on and/or potential failures that you fear. Then, for each item, write a Scripture verse that you can focus on when a weakness or failure is at the forefront of your mind.*

- *God's love casts out fear, and when he calls us to do something, he empowers us. What do you do—and what can you do—to remember God's loving and strengthening presence with you throughout the day?*

THE SURPRISING GRACE
OF INSECURITY

"It is easier for a camel to go through the eye of a
needle than for a rich person to enter the kingdom of
God." — Mark 10:25 ESV

These words of Jesus baffled and astounded his first-century listeners. Wealth was assumed to be a sign of God's blessing! By implication, those people were near—if not already in—the Lord's kingdom. What was Jesus saying?

Jesus was commenting on the very real power of money and possessions to give us a false sense of security and self-sufficiency. Ironically, God's abundant blessings can make people think they don't need him.

Elton Trueblood (1900–1994) wrote the following in *Confronting Christ*:

> *Security is itself a barrier to spiritual growth. The broken*
> *and the needy are far closer to the Kingdom than are those*
> *who feel adequate and successful. God reaches us most easily*

when there is a crack in our armor. The barriers of our own making, which effectively exclude us from the Kingdom, are real and in some cases almost insurmountable, but with God all is possible.*

Trueblood's words make me think of when a man once asked Mother Teresa to pray for him, that he would find clarity. Her response was essentially, "You don't need clarity. What you need is trust."

Security works the same way. We don't need security so much as we need trust. It is hard for the rich to enter God's kingdom because, trusting in money, they don't feel any need for the kingdom or the King. They may not even want the kingdom or want to know the King. How sad to think about what they are missing.

- *When has something, someone, or some circumstance given you a false sense of security? What broke through that illusion?*

- *What is keeping you from trusting God and entrusting yourself to God today? Take a moment to acknowledge the first five examples of God's faithfulness that come to mind—and let those encourage you to trust him in this day.*

* Elton Trueblood, *Confronting Christ* (New York: Harper & Brothers, 1960), p. 93

WELCOMED INTO GOD'S PRESENCE

I, through the abundance of your steadfast love, will enter your house, I will bow down toward your holy temple in awe of you. Lead me, O LORD, in your righteousness because of my enemies; make your way straight before me. — *Psalm 5:7–8 NRSV*

Drawing near to God and entering his house used to be reserved for only the privileged few. Only the priests were allowed, and they went through elaborate cleansing rites beforehand. I wonder if we in the twenty-first century might be helped by a little more of that kind of reverence and awe when we approach God in corporate worship and personal prayer.

This psalm gives us a starting point for recovering that reverence and awe. It might be good to consider how—on what basis—we enter the Lord's house. Do we enter because of our worthiness? Do we stay away because of our unworthiness? If we are thinking about worthiness, we may be focusing on the wrong thing. Let's shift our attention to God.

"I will enter your house *through the abundance of your steadfast love.*" What an encouraging phrase! As if God's love for us
isn't amazing enough, David adds the modifier "steadfast" and
multiplies that by "abundance." May we be overwhelmed by
God's love for us and grateful that he welcomes us, just as we
are, into his presence. May we learn to bow before our God in
awe of him and his abundant, steadfast love for us.

- *Are there ways you might sometimes be too casual or too
  formal when you approach God? Describe.*

- *What will you do to enter God's presence—both in corporate worship and in personal prayer and meditation—with
  a heart full of awe?*

CALLING ON THE LORD

Out of my distress I called on the LORD; the LORD
answered me and set me in a broad place.
— Psalm 118:5 NRSV

How do you respond to times of distress? Do you complain to those close to you? Do you find yourself calling out to the Lord? In my experience—not surprisingly—the second response has been far more fruitful than the first. After all, the promise is there: "The LORD answered me."

Our calling out won't be in vain. God's answer is sure. And his answer is an action: he puts us "in a broad place." The Book of Common Prayer (BCP) renders the second line of Psalm 118:5 as "The Lord answered by setting me free." Setting that alongside the "broad place," we can see that freedom and spaciousness go together.

Yet some of us might be surprised to realize that we're actually afraid of true freedom. Spaciousness can make us feel exposed rather than safe. We sometimes actually prefer our closed-in, constricted spaces because they provide a false sense of security. But safety and security are not so much a matter of being separated *from* danger as being protected *in* danger.

And the next verse of Psalm 118 addresses exactly that: "With the LORD on my side I do not fear. What can mortals do to me?" (v. 6 NRSV). By God's grace, a broad and spacious place is at the same time a place where we are protected and led by our Good Shepherd.

- *What past experience or current situation came to mind when you read "out of my distress"? And what did God do to bring you out of that distress—or what are you praying he will do for you now?*

- *Are you threatened by the spaciousness of true freedom? Why or why not? If so, what comfort do you find in Psalm 118:6?*

WHERE TO FIND HELP

It is better to take refuge in the Lord than to put any
confidence in flesh. It is better to take refuge in the
Lord than to put any confidence in princes.
— *Psalm 118:8–9 BCP*

Better. It's a word of comparison. It says that one thing is more helpful, more useful, more fruitful, more beneficial than another thing.

It's nice to have human reasons to be confident about our ability to do life. I am, for instance, grateful for education, natural abilities, experience, and physical resources that God has graciously and generously given me. But none of these is really a refuge from what attacks my soul. I can't buy my way out of the enemy's assaults with any amount of money. My King, the Lord, is truly a far better refuge than anything mere human resources (i.e., "the flesh") can offer.

As for putting confidence in princes, I've often been tempted to think, *If only our nonprofit had more major donors, then our troubles would be over.* That's one version of wanting to trust in princes. But my refuge and the source of my provision are really in the Lord, the Prince of Peace, who has decided to have me on his side. I haven't any lack of resources in him.

Frankly, I'm not always so clear about how to access resources God is making available. I know how to write a check or use a debit card to access funds in our bank account. I know how to pull cash out of my wallet to purchase something. But I'm still learning how to access divine resources. We can ask God to teach us how to access his resources. We can welcome him to mentor us in living and working from a place of divine provision. What a great way to pray!

- *What is your personal version of putting your trust in mere human resources (i.e., "the flesh")? What is your version of putting confidence in princes? Why do you seek confidence and trust in these lesser things? What can you do to loosen their grip on your imagination?*

- *In what ways have you experienced the generous provision of God in your life? What helped you access his resources? Why not have a prayerful conversation with God about this today.*

OUR FATHER'S RESOURCES

See what kind of love the Father has given to us, that
we should be called children of God; and so we are.
— 1 John 3:1 ESV

I'm still learning how to access the abundance of God as a child of God. As a son of my heavenly Father, I have access to all the grace and goodness he provides. I know this and am growing to rely on the abundance my Good Shepherd provides.

Prompted by that thought, I wondered, *What if I pray? What if I ask the Father plainly and with trust for what I need right now? Isn't this what Jesus has told us to do?*

Jesus did indeed teach this, and he did so with a vivid word picture—an analogy—that even those who aren't parents can appreciate:

> *"Ask, and it will be given you; search, and you will find;*
> *knock, and the door will be opened for you. For everyone*
> *who asks receives, and everyone who searches finds, and for*

everyone who knocks, the door will be opened. Is there anyone among you who, if your child asks for bread, will give a stone? Or if the child asks for a fish, will give a snake? If you then, who are evil, know how to give good gifts to your children, how much more will your Father in heaven give good things to those who ask him!" (Matt. 7:7–11 NRSV)

Ask. Search. Knock. These are words Jesus uses to talk about praying. My Father in heaven will not be stingier with me, his child, than I have been with my own sons. In fact, Jesus promised, "Your Father in heaven [will] give good gifts to those who ask him" (Matt. 7:11 NIV). Prayer is a relational encounter with a loving Father. It is asking. It is searching. It is knocking. And, thankfully, prayer leads us to places of receiving, finding, and entering in.

- *What has been causing you distress lately? How have you been praying about this source of distress? For what have you been asking and searching?*

- *Rather than first thinking about how you want God to change your situation, what might God give you, in your own soul, that would help you in this situation?*

GLAD RIVERS

We will not fear, though the earth should change,
though the mountains shake in the heart of the sea;
though its waters roar and foam, though the moun-
tains tremble with its tumult. There is a river whose
streams make glad the city of God, the holy habitation
of the Most High. — Psalm 46:2–4 NRSV

Change, especially unpleasant change, can provoke fear in us by questioning our feelings of certainty and security. Storms instead of calm, tumult instead of peace—and for who knows how long—may cause us to tremble emotionally and even spiritually. It is into such a context that this peaceful river of Psalm 46 comes into view, its streams making God's city (and my heart) glad.

There *is* a river. Have you noticed the presence of these glad rivers in your life? I think of the many days I spent as a child playing alongside the American River in Sacramento, California. There was a park right on the riverbank just a short bike ride away from my house. I spent hours there throwing rocks in the water, watching rafters float by, looking for lizards. It was a glad river full of glad memories.

I also have glad memories about the spiritual rivers in my life. God has not let me be swept away by the rapids of change. He has enabled me to test the waters with my foot, watch and learn from others who have handled the whitewater, and catch signs of his presence with me. In the places where I'm tempted to fear, I am invited to live my life next to holy streams that will refresh and delight me.

- *Spiritually speaking, describe a storm of change you have experienced. In what ways did you experience your Good Shepherd's presence, even his gladness, despite any fears that were provoked?*

- *What lessons have you learned and/or what glad memories can you recall from time spent by a spiritual river of gladness? Notice what stories the Spirit might bring to mind.*

OVERCOMING FEAR

*"Fear not, for I am with you; be not dismayed, for I
am your God." — Isaiah 41:10 ESV*

The command to "fear not" appears hundreds of times in
Scripture. God knows our human tendency to fear, or he
wouldn't have offered such reassurance again and again and
again.

But there is no simple switch to flip for sure obedience to this
often-repeated command—at least, I haven't found one yet!
Something I have found helpful, though, comes from spiritual
director and pastor Reginald Somerset Ward in *A Guide for
Spiritual Directors*. Hear his simple but potent insight about
what cures fear:

> *In considering fear, there is only one medicine which can
> produce an absolute cure; and that is a complete and over-
> whelming faith and simple trust in the love and power of
> God, in His will and ability to make of every happening in
> life a means of ultimate welfare and happiness.**

* pp. 19–20

Where faith is growing, fear diminishes. Trust—choosing to trust—in the reliable care and mighty capability of God leaves less and less room for fear that hinders, let alone fear that paralyzes. Trust in the love of God displaces fear. God really *is* working in everything—even our current circumstances—with an eye for our good and for the fulfilling of his good purposes.

- *What value do you find in a prayer like "I believe; help my unbelief" (Mark 9:24)?*

- *What has responding in trust to God's love and power looked like in your life? In what way might God be inviting you to a place of deeper, simpler trust?*

TALKING BACK TO GOD

Who are you, a human being, to talk back to God?
"Shall what is formed say to the one who formed it,
'Why did you make me like this?'" Does not the potter
have the right to make out of the same lump of clay
some pottery for special purposes and some for com-
mon use? — Romans 9:20–21 NIV

Read Paul's first question again. Do you find it a bit jarring? I do. We live in a day when the average person doesn't seem to hesitate to "talk back to God." We have rights! We deserve freedom of speech, freedom to gather, and freedom to talk back to God!

Paul's point, however, is that since God has made us, do we—that which is made—have the right to talk back to the Maker? Paul says no. What if you were a potter? Wouldn't you feel free to make special pottery and common pottery as you saw fit? Can you imagine a common pot saying, "Hey, you didn't make me special enough!" or a fine pot saying, "I would have preferred a simple existence of daily use by people. I don't like sitting on a shelf just being admired."

Note that Paul doesn't appear to be talking about the holy model of lament or complaint we see in the Psalms, but about a strident, self-willed contention with God. God welcomes our honest doubts and questions. Talking back to God is different. It's a way of placing my sense of reality above God's. I call into question his good intention and his good work in and around me. The reality of my own weaknesses, shortcomings, failures, and nearsightedness might enable me to realize that I just don't have as much perspective as God does. It's humbling but true.

Still, I'm tempted. I'm learning that no matter how I view my life or circumstances at present, I have a God who is fully loving and merciful, fully mighty and sovereign, and still fully God.

- *When we confess our shortcomings and line-crossings, God is faithful to forgive us. Take a few minutes now to acknowledge and confess pride, lack of trust, or anything else that has tempted you to talk back to God.*

- *What words describing God's nature would be most helpful to you in any places of resistance or reaction that rise up within you? (e.g., loving, merciful, gracious, mighty, sovereign)*

- *What questions might God be asking you these days?*

CHOSEN AND BELOVED

As [God] says in Hosea: "I will call them 'my people'
who are not my people; and I will call her 'my loved
one' who is not my loved one." — Romans 9:25,
quoting Hosea 2:23 NIV

God includes me among "his people" even though I was not born among his people. He calls me "beloved" even though I did not grow up knowing myself as one of his beloved. And he loved me in my childhood when I was still unaware of his presence with me. God chose me when I felt unchosen.

God wanted (and wants) me as one of his own. That is humbling and amazing to me. I have been adopted to be God's son. When I stop and think about this, I am awestruck and speechless.

But to be honest—and I'm guessing this won't surprise you—I don't always *feel* beloved by God. But feelings like these are usually rooted in an obsessive focus on my failings, which seem to say I'm not nearly as lovable as I wish. When I get to the point where I am no longer staring at myself but instead gazing at the blinding beauty, the sheer goodness, the deep love of God, then I am more able to *feel* and *trust* my beloved-ness. I long to know and trust this belovedness in the depths of my heart more and more. Perhaps this is your hunger and thirst as well.

- *What, if anything, tempts you to feel less than beloved by God? How might you be focusing on these obstacles more than on the loving face of God shining on you?*

- *Spend five or ten minutes sitting with and savoring the truth of God's fatherly words to you: "[Name], you are my beloved child."*

SERVICE: PRESENCE FOR THE SAKE OF OTHERS

"Whoever serves me must follow me, and where I am, there will my servant be also. Whoever serves me, the Father will honor." — John 12:26 NRSV

The servant of Jesus *must* be a follower of Jesus. That's what Jesus is saying here. There is no serving Jesus without following Jesus, but I have certainly tried at times.

Too often, we may try to do good things *for* Jesus while, strangely, keeping our distance *from* him. How can we be part of his kingdom work without staying in close touch with the King? Imagine a self-proclaimed ambassador seeking to represent a nation without ever having so much as a conversation with its president? The ambassador might do amazing things, but who knows whether or not she is actually representing the will and purposes of the president.

Service requires following *and* presence. And it's not hard both to know Jesus' presence and to follow Him, our Good

Shepherd, because Jesus wants that too. In fact, he promises it: "Where I am, there will my servant be also."

Think of how the Gospels show us the impact of Jesus' presence in the lives of those he taught and healed, as he provided needs and cared for those society treated as outcasts. With the very Spirit of Jesus residing in us, our presence in people's lives can also make a difference. We can express Jesus' sacrificial love by making time to be with a shut-in. We can heal broken hearts by loving the lonely and rejected. We can take a meal when a baby is born or when a loved one dies. We can love those who are treated as outcasts by serving at a homeless shelter, a suicide hotline, or a neighborhood gathering.

Serving God means being in his presence for the sake of others.

- *Where are you serving now? Think about formal ways you serve as well as informal ways. What difference will it make if you consider that service as Jesus being present in you and being present to others through you?*

- *Who has been the presence of Jesus in your life? Make time to say thank you to them.*

SEEING JESUS

[Some Greeks] came to Philip, who was from Beth-saida in Galilee, and asked him, "Sir, we wish to see Jesus." — John 12:21 ESV

I remember visiting what many archaeologists believe to be the ruins of Bethsaida, just off the northeast shore of the Sea of Galilee. We saw what some people had called "the fisher-man's house," and it easily could have been the home of Philip, one of Jesus' disciples who hailed from that village.

In John 12, some Greeks approached Philip while he was in Jerusalem for the Passover feast. I love their request: "we wish to see Jesus." My desire resonates with theirs. I want to see Jesus in the faces of my family, my friends, and those I serve. I want to see Jesus in my relationships. I want to see Jesus in my work. I want to see Jesus in the beauty of creation. I want to see Jesus when circumstances are dark, discouraging, or overwhelming.

I feel that deep hunger to have a clearer and more intimate vision of Jesus in every facet of my life. I get into the most trouble when my vision of Jesus grows faint or blurry. Lord, open my eyes wider to see you more clearly.

- *When has seeing Jesus made a difference in your interaction with family members, a friend, a neighbor, or someone in your workplace? What indicated to you that Jesus was present with you?*

- *What are you doing—and what could you do—either on your own or with a good friend, to gain and maintain a clearer and more intimate vision of Jesus? Be encouraged that he wants that for you too.*

THE COURAGE OF SERVANTHOOD

*Jesus, knowing that the Father had given all things
into his hands, and that he had come from God and
was going back to God, rose from supper. He laid aside
his outer garments, and taking a towel, tied it around
his waist. — John 13:3–4 ESV*

Truly serving others is empowered by the confidence of secure provision and holy belonging. Jesus served from a place of abundance and confidence. His service was an expression of strength, not weakness. Holy service is like that.

Although not one of the disciples had humbled himself and taken on this servant's task, Jesus got on his knees to wash twenty-four dusty feet. When he got to Peter, the former fisherman objected to the Rabbi washing his feet. But Jesus was firm: "If I do not wash you, you have no share with me" (John 13:8).

I empathize with Peter. It would feel absolutely wrong for Jesus to wash my feet. If anyone should be washing feet, that person should be me and the feet should be his.

But Jesus reminds me that his humble act of serving was relational, not just functional. Impulsive Peter's "You will never wash my feet" is really him saying no to the wishes and will of Jesus. Jesus wanted Peter to have a heart more willing to trust that he had good reason for what he was doing.

Jesus comes to you today, serving you from a place of loving authority. He would stoop to wash your feet. His service would be a way for you to become his follower in the service of others. What might that look like today?

- *When, if ever, have you been surprised by someone's act of service to you or to someone else? What did God teach you in that experience?*

- *When were you faced with a task that felt too messy, too difficult, or too humiliating for you to take on? How did you respond? Would you respond differently now if the same opportunity arose for you? In light of Jesus washing the disciples' feet, how would you like to pray? What would you like to talk with Jesus about?*

AUTHORITY THAT SERVES

"The kings of the Gentiles lord it over them; and
those who exercise authority over them call themselves
Benefactors. But you are not to be like that. Instead,
the greatest among you should be like the youngest,
and the one who rules like the one who serves."
— *Luke 22:25–26 NIV*

Human rulers who do not serve under the kingdom of God demand attention, expect special and exceptional treatment, and require their will to be obeyed without question. They do not come to serve but to *be* served. They want to be admired and respected, if not fawned over. Jesus said that none of this should mark the character of servants in his kingdom.

In contrast, King Jesus invites his servants—you and me—to give attention to the needs of others. He wants God's purpose and his love to be our focus. In fact, in Jesus' kingdom, his people—you and I—really are called to practice service. We may be tempted to think of ourselves as being above certain others, whether consciously or subconsciously. We might try to serve others from this perceived elevated place, but God wants us to remember that we are all people in need of grace.

In kingdom service, we don't seek anyone's admiration or accolades. We learn to point to Jesus in all we do so that the people we serve in his name will admire him and not us.

- *Why is it hard for us to serve for God's glory instead of for recognition from others?*

- *Can you think of an act of service (your own or another's) where the focus really was on an awareness of God's presence and not on the person serving? What did that look like? What did it feel like?*

STRONG TO SERVE

*And now the LORD says—he who formed me in the
womb to be his servant to bring Jacob back to him
and gather Israel to himself, for I am honored in the
eyes of the LORD and my God has been my strength.*
— Isaiah 49:5 NIV

In this verse, the Old Testament prophet Isaiah was talking about his calling, about his kingdom mission. In all that this calling demanded from Isaiah, the prophet writes that God has been his strength.

In my own calling and kingdom mission, God has proven to be *my* strength as well. I am so grateful for ways in which I am learning to rely on divine strength in my own felt sense of weakness. I long to work from this place of kingdom grace, gentleness, and humility. And the world around me needs whatever it is that God wishes to do through me. That could easily sound self-important, but this really doesn't have a great deal to do with me. *God* is my strength. *God* is the One with the purpose, the ability to guide me, and the design to use me as he wishes.

I feel a connection to Isaiah's mission of bringing God's people back to him so that through them, the entire world might come to know the true God. God called Isaiah to be a light to those who are not yet God's people so that they, too, might see how life in God is available to them and gives them a purpose for existence.

God is inviting you into this work as well. God will give you strength to fulfill this invitation if you want to respond to it.

- *I feel called like Isaiah was: to bring God's people back to him. In what ways does this calling resonate with you? How would you describe your sense of calling from God? If you're not sure, make it a topic of prayer over the next few weeks. Ask God's Spirit to give you insight.*

- *If you already have a sense of your calling, what next steps does God seem to be inviting you to take?*

- *When have you sensed God providing his strength and enabling you to do what he called you to do? How did you recognize that it was the Lord's strength?*

FORMED TO BE HIS SERVANT

*[The LORD] formed me in the womb to be his servant
to bring Jacob back to him and gather Israel to himself, for I am honored in the eyes of the LORD and my
God has been my strength. — Isaiah 49:5 NIV*

Early in this verse, Isaiah referred to the Lord as "he who formed me in the womb to be his servant." It's hard for me to believe, at one level, that I was formed in my mother Shirley's womb to be God's servant. My mother may not have been aware of God's purposes at the time in the way that Mary clearly was about her son, Jesus. But before I was even born, I had already been chosen . . . by God.

When I was four years old, anxious and fearful as so many little ones are, I was already chosen. When I was eleven and seeking to find some sense of meaning in a more and more perfect academic performance, I was already chosen. When I was thirteen and mercilessly teased by popular kids in junior high, I was already chosen. And when I was seventeen, desperately indulging in any pleasure I could find, I was already chosen. None of those rather big bumps in my journey changed that I was chosen.

I feel humbled. I feel grateful. I also feel nervous, anxious, fearful, self-doubting, and insecure. At the same time that I experience these emotional echoes of something old, I am coming to trust and feel the honor of being chosen. I was wanted by God even before I was wanted by my own mother.

- *What does it mean to you that God has chosen you to recognize Jesus as your Savior and to be a member of his family forever? How does this reality impact your day-to-day life?*

- *Are you feeling the honor of having been chosen by God? If so, how? If not, how might you enter into this very fitting response to God's gracious act?*

BEING FAITHFUL TO GOD

Test me, O Lord, and try me; examine my heart
and my mind. For your love is before my eyes; I have
walked faithfully with you. — Psalm 26:2–3 BCP

Unlike David, the writer of this psalm, I don't always feel the same confidence to be able to go before the Lord and state without qualification, "I have walked faithfully with you." Why? Because I'm painfully aware of how I am sometimes unfaithful.

Maybe I could place the Lord's love before my eyes instead. I could imagine the face of God smiling with favor. I could envision his pleasure over me as his child. I could trust that his love is always greater than my shortcomings.

Maybe I could ask God to "examine my heart and my mind" and talk with me about my faithfulness and how it might grow. What might he say to me? Perhaps this:

You have let yourself become discouraged by your weakness
when you could be encouraged by, and reliant on, my gra-

cious strength and faithfulness. You have let yourself be intimidated by empty fears when you might walk in the courage of my protective, mighty presence.

Take time to refresh your vision of me day by day, even moment by moment. Receive and welcome my presence, my power, my vision, my mission for your life. Step into the promise I have given you. I will be with you as you do your work. Abide in me as you do this good work I have given you to do. Let's do it together, beginning right now.

Maybe I can just let my small faithfulness reflect God's great faithfulness to me.

- *On a scale of 1 to 10, how confident are you in saying to God "I have walked faithfully with you"? Explain why you answered as you did. Comment, too, on what makes that proclamation easy or difficult.*

- *Why might God's faithful presence with you be key to your being faithful to him?*

GRACE AND PEACE: THE ABUNDANT BASICS

May grace and peace be yours in abundance in the
knowledge of God and of Jesus our Lord.
— 2 Peter 1:2 NRSV

So many New Testament letters begin with a prayer that "grace and peace" will be with the recipients. I like that this good, basic reality is the starting point. After all, we very much need God's grace, manifested in his generous and empowering presence, among other things. We also need the deep well-being and wholeness that God's peace brings to us.

The apostle Peter wanted his readers then and now to experience both abundant grace and abundant peace, and Peter realized that grace and peace are rooted in our personal experiential knowledge of God and our Lord Jesus. This abundance is not just for our own benefit but is also for the sake of others, as implied in Peter's words below:

You must make every effort to support your faith with goodness, and goodness with knowledge, and knowledge with self-control, and self-control with endurance, and endurance with godliness, and godliness with mutual affection, and mutual affection with love. (2 Peter 1:5–7 NRSV)

How good it is—for us and for those around us—as we become people characterized by faith in God, goodness, self-control, affection, and love.

- *What would you say if someone asked you to explain what grace—specifically God's grace—is? Spend some time finding a way to talk about grace that is more natural for you and that people new to the concept would understand.*

- *Share two or three ways you have found greater grace and peace coming from your growing personal experiential knowledge of God and of our Lord Jesus. Comment on why grace and (perhaps especially) peace increase as we know Jesus better.*

EVERYTHING WE NEED

His divine power has given us everything needed for
life and godliness, through the knowledge of him who
called us by his own glory and goodness.
— 2 Peter 1:3 NRSV

I love the rhythm between "has given us everything needed"
here in verse 3 and "you must make every effort to support
your faith with" that comes in verse 5.

This passage contains such a wonderful promise! God's people are abundantly supplied to be able to work hard for God's
glory with confidence and effectiveness. The confidence and
effectiveness come because we know that our efforts are fully
supported by all the resources we need for the tasks of life and
for godliness.

In other words, I do not need to wait for resources to do the
work God has given me to do. Our never-changing God has
given his people who went before us everything they needed
for life and godliness, and he won't stop doing so for you or
me. God promises his resources, but they may not fall from

the heavens effortlessly like manna. We may be required to do some patient farming before we are able to draw on those abundant resources.

We can count on God to enable us to work persistently and wait patiently for that farming to bear fruit. Then we can be good stewards of the good harvest that comes.

- *When has God surprised you with unexpectedly abundant provisions, either in the work you were doing for him or in your pursuit of godliness? Comment on that experience or another that you have witnessed.*

- *What fruit—what resources for life and godliness—are you waiting to come as a result of some farming? Or maybe it's seed-sowing time. What do you think God wants you to do to access the resources he promises?*

GRACE AND DISCIPLINE: INVESTING OUR TIME

For everything there is a season, and a time for every matter under heaven: a time to be born, and a time to die. — *Ecclesiastes 3:1–2 ESV*

God invites us to show our love for him and for people by obeying his commands and serving according to his loving call in our lives. He gives us the resources we will need as well as peace and grace.

Yet God's generous empowerment doesn't come to me as I sit around inactive and disengaged. The engine of grace requires the transmission of my engaged will. In prayer, for instance, I actively welcome grace into every relationship and activity of my life. As Reginald Somerset Ward says in *A Guide for Spiritual Directors*, we actively welcome grace into our life by spending the currency of our time:

> *Grace requires for its use and fruition our cooperation, which is given by the soul through its authentic voice, the will, in the*

form of discipline. Discipline in prayer is expressed by paying the cost of receiving and developing the grace. If we search for the manner in which this cost must be paid, it would seem that there is only one universal currency common to all human beings in the world, and that is the amount of time between the present moment and the moment of our death. It seems likely that, in the last analysis, every human desire has to be paid for in this currency. (pp. 50–51)

Everything we involve ourselves in, we pay for with the currency of time. What I do with my time determines the outcome of my life. I want to be a person who spends my time well. I want to learn where I am spending it unwisely. I want every moment of every day to be invested well. What am I investing my time in for the long-term? And why in the world would I ever want to *kill* time?

- *Where are you wasting time? What do you spend your time on from day to day? What are you investing your time in for the long-term?*

- *What course of action do your answers to the preceding three questions suggest?*

A FAMILY RESEMBLANCE

*[Jesus] was told, "Your mother and your brothers are
standing outside, desiring to see you." But he answered
them, "My mother and my brothers are those who
hear the word of God and do it."*
— *Luke 8:20–21 ESV*

Some people are better than others at recognizing family resemblances. To be honest, when looking at a newborn, I often
can't say whose nose he has. But some family resemblances
simply can't be missed—and I'm not just talking about identi-
cal twins. At times I am able to see, without a doubt, which
parent's nose or eyes or hair a baby has!

It can also be good to look at resemblances that go beyond
physical features. For instance, a mother and daughter who
speak in the same unique cadence and tone of voice, or a father
and son who laugh the same way or walk with the same gait.

Family resemblances can be uncanny and even unexpected.
Consider that Jesus acknowledged as family those who were
following his counsel and embodying his love. That kind of

behavior is what makes for a family-of-God resemblance in you and in me. To the degree that I am living according to Jesus' counsel and commands, he would say, "Alan is my brother." I'm stunned by that sentence: "Alan is my brother." But the converse is also true. I am not living as Jesus' brother if I live my life or conduct myself in ways that do not honor him.

Think about what character traits and regular actions reveal the reality that you are a child of God—and which traits and actions don't express this reality.

- *Put your name in the blank as you imagine Jesus saying: "_____ is my brother/sister." Read the sentence silently as well as aloud, noting your emotions. Were you stunned? What did you feel?*

- *What can you do that may help this truth penetrate your mind and heart?*

"WHO IS THIS?"

[Jesus] said to [his disciples], "Where is your faith?"
They were afraid and amazed, and said to one an-
other, "Who then is this, that he commands even the
winds and the water, and they obey him?"
— Luke 8:25 NRSV

Maybe you've sensed Jesus asking you at one time or another, "Where is your faith?" He asks with kindness and grace, but still he asks. Life can shake our faith. The unexpected, the injustices, the diagnosis, the disarray, the consequences of sin (our own and that which others commit against us), the low bank account, the high expectations—many things can cause storms in our lives. And yes, our faith is often shaken and sometimes feels completely blown away.

But maybe, like the disciples, you've seen Jesus calm a storm in your life. Maybe you also have been prompted to ask, "Who is this?" This is the incarnate Lord and Creator of everything, able to walk the ground of his own creation and be present with those who call him Savior and Lord.

As today unfolds, let's be alert for situations that are actually invitations to rest in Jesus. Let's receive challenging circumstances as opportunities to gently trust in him. When we do, we will find peace from the internal storm, if not from the external circumstances. May we sense Jesus' companionship throughout the day.

- *Consider a past storm that you saw Jesus calm. If you didn't see his hand in the moment, maybe you can see it more clearly looking back. What were the circumstances? What was the resolution? What impact did this experience have on your faith?*

- *What storm currently rages in your life? In what ways is the Lord at work calming the waves and wind?*

HE HOLDS YOUR HAND

*"I, the LORD, have called you in righteousness; I will
take hold of your hand." — Isaiah 42:6 NIV*

"I will take hold of your hand." That everyday action can be
profoundly significant. I can still remember the first time I
reached over and held Gem's hand on one of our early dates.
Suddenly the two of us knew that the relationship had reached
a new level and that our roles might be redefined a bit. The
amount of time we spent together grew. I began to think that
she might be more than my present girlfriend; she might be
my future wife.

That everyday action of holding hands can also be a gift of
safety and security. At a scary movie, it is nice to have a hand
to hold. When you are responsible for a child's safety, it is
critical to hold hands in a crowd, in a parking lot, and when
crossing a street. In reading these first lines of Isaiah 42:6, I
imagined a good father taking hold of his young son's hand to
guide him, protect him, encourage him, and be a companion
to him.

Our heavenly Father has promised to take hold of our hand—to guide us, protect us, encourage us, and be a companion to us. May we be grateful when we sense—or when we choose to trust—that God has taken our hand today. After all, next to our heavenly Father, the Ancient of Days, each of us is indeed a little child.

- *God can reach to take your hand, but do you always reach back? What has kept you from taking your Good Shepherd's hand?*

- *Remember a time when God took hold of your hand. What difference did it make to your internal world? How did you feel as you reached back to take his hand?*

"I WILL KEEP YOU"

"I will keep you and will make you to be a covenant
for the people and a light for the Gentiles, to open
eyes that are blind, to free captives from prison and to
release from the dungeon those who sit in darkness."
— *Isaiah 42:6–7 NIV*

This is quite an invitation God has for us, his people! As daunting as the details might be, notice the starting point: "I will keep you." Whatever aspect of God's invitation we are responding to, and whatever our anxieties and concerns, that promise can make all the difference.

The Lord will keep you—the Lord will keep me—and enable us to help those who don't yet know him. God will use us to love those who are spiritually blind and cause his love to shine through us so they can see him. God will use us to love those who are trapped in past sin and help them find the freedom of forgiveness, deliverance, and hope. God will use us to love those who sit in dark prisons—of their own making or made by others—and help them recognize the light of his truth.

We live in a time when many people in our sphere of influence are spiritually blind and imprisoned, even though they consider themselves completely sighted and free. God invites us to offer him our time, our energy, and our hearts for the good of those he brings into our lives. What a gift. What an honor.

- *Whom did God use in your life to help your blind eyes see, to free you from prison, and to bring you into the light of his truth? Thank him for the family members, friends, authors, mentors, or perhaps life circumstances that he used to work these changes in you.*

- *What, if anything, keeps you from responding more fully to your Good Shepherd so he can use you in this important kingdom work? What can and will you do to overcome those barriers?*

HOW THE FIRST CHRISTIANS DID CHURCH, PART 1

They devoted themselves to the apostles' teaching and
to fellowship, to the breaking of bread and to prayer.
— *Acts 2:42 NIV*

I wonder if we hear this line from Acts and imagine these early Jesus-followers devoting themselves to going to Bible study, church meetings, potlucks, and then to an occasional prayer meeting here or there. Maybe we see the faithful or hardcore few attending a midweek prayer meeting. This verse is saying so much more, though.

First, the apostles were speaking from their eyewitness experiences and their living relationship with the risen Christ, Jesus of Nazareth. They weren't simply talking about Jesus; these witnesses to the resurrected Lord were sharing Jesus' life with other followers.

Also, the idea of fellowship gets unpacked in this passage as meaning so much more than simply attending meetings:

All the believers were together and had everything in common. They sold property and possessions to give to anyone who had need. Every day they continued to meet together in the temple courts. (Acts 2:44–46 NIV)

These early followers of Jesus were together and shared what they had with one another. Some even sold their property or possessions to meet the needs of their brothers and sisters. There was much less a sense of "mine and yours" and much more a sense of "ours."

Also, the "breaking of bread" was more than just eating meals together. It was sharing together in a time of being spiritually nourished at the table Christ gave us: "They broke bread in their homes and ate together with glad and sincere hearts" (Acts 2:46). What a beautiful family photo!

- *What details in the Acts 2:42 description of the early church might prompt the world to take notice? Why?*

- *In what ways does your community in Christ reflect the early church's way of living together in Christ? How might you all take new steps together?*

HOW THE FIRST CHRISTIANS DID CHURCH, PART 2

They devoted themselves to the apostles' teaching and to fellowship, to the breaking of bread and to prayer.
— *Acts 2:42 NIV*

Devoted. *Devoted* to God and his ways . . .

I sometimes feel semi-devoted. And I sometimes feel alone in my devotion. How about you? When I think about devotion to God, I too often think "me" and not "us." I wonder if this isn't an unfortunate fruit of our modern, hurried world.

But I can't excuse myself by blaming some faceless "them," can I? A better option is to acknowledge that I feel both hungry for and resistant to the level of community and mutual engagement I see in this first Christian community.

A greater sense of community and mutual engagement would, I think, encourage in me a devotion to prayer. I can imagine prayer becoming so much more than merely asking God for stuff or performing a religious duty. I can imagine prayer becoming a shared life of contemplative communion, filling and transforming hearts, blessing and glorifying God.

May God bless us with this heartfelt devotion to him and to his people so we may be winsome witnesses to his goodness and love, drawing others to his family.

- *What can we do to fuel our devotion to God? Think about people through history and about people you know personally who are radiantly devoted to God. Learn from them— and even interview the people you know!*

- *Do you experience much "us-ness" in your prayer life? If not, find a prayer partner or a small group that makes prayer an important component or even the main reason for meeting.*

HOW GOOD AND PLEASANT!

How good and pleasant it is when God's people live
together in unity! ... It is as if the dew of Hermon
were falling on Mount Zion. For there the LORD
bestows his blessing, even life forevermore.
— Psalm 133:1, 3 NIV

It is indeed good and pleasant when people—especially God's people—dwell in unity. When people are of one mind for a specific goal—when God's people are of one heart overflowing with love for him and for one another—good things can happen.

In the same way, it isn't very good or very pleasant when our human brokenness divides us or distances us from one another. Instead of feeling like the "dew of Hermon," it feels more like the deserts of Sinai.

In this psalm, David acknowledges the unexpected beauty of unity when he refers to Mount Hermon and Mount Zion.

The temperate climate of Hermon meant green lushness, and David imagined Hermon's fresh dew falling in the desert-like climate of Mount Zion. The life-giving and perhaps somewhat surprising relief of that morning dew would indeed be good and pleasant for residents of Mount Zion.

Zion is God's dwelling place. It's the place where God offers his blessing of life forevermore. God invites you to be part of the work of bringing his people together. As we each draw near to him individually, we'll find that we are drawing close to one another as well. How good and pleasant it is.

- *If you've ever traveled to Israel, think back to what you saw of Mount Hermon and Mount Zion. (If you haven't, take a moment to do a web search about those two locations.) What richness does this experience add to your reading of Psalm 133?*

- *When has God given you unexpected refreshment in a desert season of your life? How can that touchstone encourage you if life is a bit desert-like right now?*

GRACE-INSPIRED GENEROSITY

Soon afterward he went on through cities and villages, proclaiming and bringing the good news of the kingdom of God. And the twelve were with him, and also some women who had been healed of evil spirits and infirmities: Mary, called Magdalene, from whom seven demons had gone out, and Joanna, the wife of Chuza, Herod's household manager, and Susanna, and many others, who provided for them out of their means. — Luke 8:1–3 ESV

Did you notice the last phrase of this passage? "Who provided for them out of their means." Yes, Jesus and the Twelve relied on the support of people who were committed to following him and learning from him. Many of their primary supporters were women who had each benefitted from Jesus' healing ministry and now travelled with him and the disciples.

Blessed by God's gracious healing, these women provided financial support so that others would benefit from Jesus' healing and teaching and grace. Even today, people who partner with a kingdom ministry will often be those who have benefitted from the grace of that ministry. We have experienced that in Unhurried Living. We have seen that when people are blessed by God through what we offer them, they often partner with us to further the reach of our ministry.

In other words, our ministry partners receive before they give. We give what we have of kingdom grace, and they give what they have, including financial support. We do indeed serve God and his people together.

Jesus freely gave what he had, and some people freely gave back what they had.

- *What new perspective or fresh encouragement did you receive from today's reading? How might God be stirring you to some next step of response?*

- *God blesses us, his people, so that we can be a blessing to others (see Gen. 12:2–3). In what ways have you been able to be a blessing because of God's blessings to you? Think specifically. And what additional blessings did you experience as a result of giving?*

THE BREAD OF LIFE

"I am the living bread that came down from heaven.
Whoever eats of this bread will live forever; and the
bread that I will give for the life of the world is my
flesh." — John 6:51 NRSV

When Jesus was tempted by Satan in the wilderness, the enemy challenged him to turn stones into bread. Jesus responded, "Man shall not live on bread alone, but on every word that comes from the mouth of God" (Matt. 4:4 NIV).

In his ministry, Jesus—the Son of God, completely man and completely God—gave us words of life. Jesus himself feeds and nourishes me. He is the One from the heavens who gives himself to me so that I might truly live an abundant life as I walk with him on this earth, as well as an eternal life of joy, freedom, and wholeness in heaven. Every other "good life" the world proposes is nothing compared to the goodness of life lived with Jesus.

But some people simply do not accept this idea. For example, some of the Jews who heard Jesus teach complained, "Is this not Jesus, the son of Joseph, whose father and mother we know? How can he now say, 'I came down from heaven'?" (John 6:42 NIV). They thought they knew Jesus because they had watched him grow up. They believed they knew exactly who Jesus was because they were familiar with the facts of his earthly life. They had eyes but failed to see.

Jesus is the living bread that came down from heaven. The life of Jesus nourishes us in deep and lasting ways. Jesus invites you to take in the good words he speaks so that your soul would be well-fed today.

- *Why do some people today feel they know Jesus . . . and reject him? In other words, what false ideas about Jesus are out there, and why do they exist?*

- *What has most surprised you as you have gotten to know Jesus better through the years? Mention two or three things.*

THE NEW HAS COME

If anyone is in Christ, he is a new creation. The old
has passed away; behold, the new has come.
— *2 Corinthians 5:17 ESV*

Jesus was—and is—the Son of God and therefore truly worthy of worship, but the Jews treated him just like any other young man who had been raised among them. As I mentioned in yesterday's reading, some of the Jews thought they knew Jesus because they had watched him grow up. They hadn't seen anything divine about Jesus during those years.

Similarly, I'm guessing that many people who knew me when I was growing up wouldn't expect me to be who I am today. They might be surprised that the quiet, shy kid they knew then is now a preacher, a teacher, and an author. They might also be surprised about my commitment to follow Jesus and introduce him to those who don't yet know him.

I am not defined by the experiences I had growing up, nor am I defined by anyone who sees me only in human terms. I am now someone who is alive forever because I have been—and continue to be—nourished in soul by Jesus. His very life is feeding me so that I might grow strong for the good and glory of his kingdom. This is my reality.

If you are "in Christ" this is your reality too. Whatever your past, whatever your growing-up years were like, you are a new creation.

- *In what specific ways does Jesus, your Good Shepherd, want to feed you, quench your thirst, and give you energy for the good work that he has prepared for you?*

- *Looking back, what signs do you see in your growing-up years that hinted you would one day walk with Jesus, and/ or what evidence might have suggested otherwise?*

EAT MY FLESH, DRINK MY BLOOD, PART 1

"Just as the living Father sent me, and I live because of the Father, so whoever eats me will live because of me."
— *John 6:57 NRSV*

"Whoever eats me . . ."

Imagine hearing those words for the first time—and hearing them from a respected teacher, a man you have come to love. "Where did this idea come from," they may have wondered, "and what could it possibly mean?"

At the time, the Jews were completely confused and understandably offended by the idea of eating a human body. At that moment, however, Jesus was not speaking literally—he didn't hold out his arm for them to take a bite. But Jesus' words were also more than merely symbolic. This statement has profound meaning, as you may have discovered for yourself through your own participation in Communion.

And I hope we can come to better grasp that meaning without getting into a debate about whether the bread and the wine of Communion are the literal body and blood of Jesus. I really think that's not the point. As I see it, the point is that Jesus himself is our nourishment and our refreshment. We eat the bread and drink the cup in order to receive Jesus. Let's be nourished together by feeding on him.

- *"Jesus' words were also more than merely symbolic." Explain what that statement means to you. Refer to times when Jesus—especially through the wine and bread of Communion—has nourished you.*

- *How would you explain the meaning of Jesus' words "Whoever eats me will live because of me" to someone unacquainted with him?*

EAT MY FLESH, DRINK MY BLOOD, PART 2

"Just as the living Father sent me, and I live because of
the Father, so whoever eats me will live because of me."
— John 6:57 NRSV

Jesus is at the heart of this holy "just as" statement: according to the eternal plan of God, the Father sent Jesus the Son to live on this earth—and to die and live again on this earth. Jesus lived because of the Father's power on display in both the incarnation and the resurrection. Jesus uses the words "just as" about being sent by the living Father and living because of the Father. In the same way, those of us who eat and drink of Jesus live because of him, because of the truth he proclaimed, because of the immeasurable grace of God.

The Eucharist—also called Communion or the Lord's Table—is a corporate and visible experience of the reality that we are nourished and energized for God's work by eating and drinking of Jesus. But I am not limited to eating and drinking of Jesus only when I gather with other followers around bread and wine. I think the Twelve were eating and drinking of Jesus in those years of discipleship without once celebrating Eucharist.

Again, I try to imagine being one of the Jewish leaders standing there and hearing Jesus tell them to eat his body and drink his blood. I would have been puzzled, offended, incredulous. But Jesus was saying something important about the nature of eternal life: we enter in only through a vital, nourishing, life-giving, interactive relationship with Jesus.

- *What does it mean to you that the disciples were eating and drinking of Jesus in those years of discipleship even though they didn't celebrate the Eucharist until that last night in the upper room?*

- *In what specific ways do you eat Christ's body and drink his blood in your everyday life? What difference does that make in how you live?*

ETERNAL RULE, UNCHANGING LAWS

Your throne was established long ago; you are from all
eternity.... Your statutes, LORD, stand firm; holiness
adorns your house for endless days.
— Psalm 93:2, 5 NIV

Only two of Psalm 93's five verses are provided here, but they
are rich. Let the kingdom reality they describe soak in.

The psalmist acknowledges that God himself has ruled everything "from all eternity." He has ruled everything before there
was anything except the Triune God himself. As sovereign
and eternal God, no one established his reign for him. The
Almighty needed no help or additional authority. Nor was he
elected or appointed or named successor to someone else. God
exists from all eternity past, and he will exist throughout all
eternity future. What a remarkable truth!

Then, as verse 5 teaches, not only does God's throne—his rule—
exist from eternity past throughout eternity future, but so does
his holiness. We also see that the Lord's statutes stand firm.

I still emotionally resist the word *statute* because it reminds me of legalistic teachings and modeling from my early Christian experience. But a beautiful, simple statute that leads to fuller joy, peace, and energy for the kingdom is not something to resist. I am choosing to receive God's statutes as good news and a great opportunity to really live. He is guiding me into the place of secure and abundant life.

Finally, there are no commands in Psalm 93. The psalmist simply acknowledges God—his eternal existence, his authority over all, his holiness, and his steadfast reign.

Like the psalmist, you and I have a God who reigns and who has chosen us and adopted us as his children. We can behold God's beauty. We can approach God's eternal throne freely and confidently.

- *When have you appreciated the value of God's statutes and laws? When, for instance, did his guidelines provide you much-needed guidance, protection, wisdom, or grace?*

- *Was today's psalm a timely reminder to acknowledge God's sovereignty, wisdom, love, and power? Why? And why do we sometimes forget these truths?*

OUR GOOD SHEPHERD

"My sheep hear my voice. I know them, and they fol-
low me. I give them eternal life, and they will never
perish. No one will snatch them out of my hand."
— *John 10:27–28 NRSV*

Jesus is so matter-of-fact here. His sheep hear his voice. He knows them and they know him. He leads them and they follow him. Similarly, when we hear the voice of our Good Shepherd—when we know him as Savior, as Lord, as Friend, and when we follow where he leads—he blesses us with eternal life. We will never perish: we will not experience the eternal death that is complete separation from God. We will never die. We are alive, now and forever.

Not everyone who heard Jesus teach, however, understood his role as shepherd and their implied role as sheep. Many Jews wanted Jesus to use plain, straightforward language and tell them directly, "I am the Messiah you've been waiting for and seeking." Instead, Jesus essentially said, "I have told you what I want to say, and I have said it exactly the way I chose to say it. I know your hearts, though: I know you are determined not to believe me or to believe *in* me despite the fact that what I do has all the marks of the Father's character, power, and love."

Like the Jews of Jesus' day, we might think that plain words meeting our criteria are what we need. But Jesus gives us truth on his own terms. Rather than making demands of Jesus, we listen well so we can receive all the good he desires to give. He really is a *Good* Shepherd!

- *Why are some people (and perhaps why were you) determined not to believe in Jesus—crucified, died, and living again—and/or determined not to follow his ways?*

- *What freedoms come with receiving Jesus as God's Son and living life with him in keeping his commands and following his example?*

SECURITY IN OUR GOOD SHEPHERD

"I give them eternal life, and they will never perish.
No one will snatch them out of my hand."
— *John 10:28 NRSV*

Writing about Jesus as Good Shepherd in these pages has prompted gratitude deep within me. I feel honored to be a recipient of the Lord's friendship, wisdom, and love. The Jews of his day, however, weren't willing to believe Jesus when he called himself the bread of life, the Good Shepherd, the way to eternal life. Instead, they tried to access Jesus from a safe distance. They did not enter into the knowledge he was offering—namely, the knowledge of his friendship and of the generous grace that comes with following him. Jesus wanted to show the Jews how to *really* live as God's people; he wanted to welcome them into eternal life. But these religious people wanted to get their religious facts in order, and Jesus wasn't meeting them there.

Aren't we sometimes tempted to approach Jesus for our reasons rather than his? We may think we have the best ideas about what we need from God, but God would give us life that lasts if we would humbly listen to his counsel. He loves to lead us on paths that are just right for us.

Once we see—by God's grace—our need for this Good Shepherd, we experience the reality of security now and forever. The Good Shepherd protects us from thieves, robbers, and wolves. And we can rest in his promise that no one can snatch us out of his hand. Not now, not ever.

- *As you reflect on this last reading, how might Jesus want to be your Good Shepherd today? Is there something he wants to lead you out of? Is there something he wants to lead you more deeply into?*

- *What is it about the grace of God that has most recently touched your life? In what ways have you experienced God's kind generosity? In what ways are you hungry to taste grace in fresh ways?*

Made in the USA
Middletown, DE
13 September 2018